Meditations in Times of Wonder

MEDITATIONS
IN
TIMES OF WONDER

Michael Martin

Angelico Press

First published in the USA
by Angelico Press
© Michael Martin 2014

For information, address:
Angelico Press, Ltd.
4709 Briar Knoll Dr. Kettering, OH 45429
www.angelicopress.com

978-1-62138-078-8

Cover image: *Partie in Dresden*
(*View over the fields near Dresden*), 1830
by Johan Christian Dahl (1788–1857)
Cover design: Michael Schrauzer

CONTENTS

Acknowledgments

Some of these poems were included in a limited-edition chapbook issued by Franciscan University at Steubenville courtesy of David Craig, to whom I offer my gratitude. I also extend thanks to the editors of the following publications in which the following poems first appeared:

Chiron Review: "Death of the Hermaphrodite"
Dappled Things: "Blood and Water, Smoke and Light," "Him to the Night," and "Signs"
Eclipse: "My Father: The Wind"
Maxis Review: "Camera Obscura"
Pacific Review: "Everything you mother Buddha say"
Red Hawk Review: "Agon"
Relief: "Answer, possibly to Virgil," "It All Comes Down to Laundry," "Opticks," "Visions of Vladimir," and "Words written during the suffering and subsequent death of John Paul II, the Pope of Rome"
Saint Katherine Review: "Aubade," "Pilcrow," and "The Poetics of Space"
Scintilla: "Dat rosa mel apibus"
Tiferet: "Self-Portrait with Graveyard"

Foreword

dixitque ad eum dimitte me iam enim ascendit aurora
respondit non dimittam te nisi benedixeris mihi
—Genesis 32:27

These poems, each one individually and the collection as a whole, figure
the classic agon: Jacob wrestling with the angel, an image which is, for
me, the archetype of both the life of faith and the creative act. They
arrived over a number of years. Meteors touching the darkness, burning
in their fall. Each came forward in struggle. Each departed in blessing.

mm

Feast of the Exaltation of the Holy Cross, 2013

For Our Lady of Chartres

The Time That Remains

". . . . just as the past becomes possible again in some fashion through memory—that which was fulfilled becomes unfulfilled and the unfulfilled becomes fulfilled—so too in messianic recapitulation do men ready themselves to forever take leave of the past in eternity, which knows neither past nor repetition." ~ Giorgio Agamben

And, so, we are at the mercy
Of two different times:
That which possesses us,
Like a metronome
Acknowledging no duration
But the pulse and its
Ominous sovereignty;
And that which we possess,
Inhabiting us with
The exigency of love.
Thus theology.

When you arrived
In the autumn of my
Twenty-seventh year
The illuminated book
Of the world, dyed
In pigments of dried blood
And virgin's milk,
Adorned itself
With sapphires and fire.
In a shimmering voice
You sang of love
And of time's ending,
And I lost myself
Counting the stars in your eyes.

What is to be done
With the time that remains,
This time turned upon itself
That crumbles like the lace
Of an ancient wedding dress
As we unfold it, dropping
Pearls into our hands
That we struggle to preserve
Or at least understand,
While planets laugh in their orbits
And we are shaken free of being?

Andromeda

"And always, night and day, he was in the places of solitude, and in the tombs, crying, and cutting himself with stones."   ~ Mark 5:5

All of us inhabit places of solitude.
We live among ghosts, and in our madness
Strive for the eternal glory of punishment.
Who is the monster? Who the hero?
And who is the virgin chained to the rock
As the emerald sea churns and charcoal
Clouds scud across a pallid sky?

Every picture we paint is a self-portrait,
Every image a cipher of being.
We open our eyes and slough off
The rags of dreams only to enter
A mythology of deeper allegiances.

So in the garden the November roses
Continue to open, even after frost,
Though without the enthusiasm they
Unleashed in the heady rush of May
When the biological imperative
Compelled them to exuberance.
But they open, nonetheless, their
Essence uncompromised by
The dictates of the exacting line
And they give themselves to death
Or the possibilities of some other glory,
As a winged boy descends from the element
And tombs grow resplendent with moss.

The Poetics of Space

"This water becomes essential; and the power of the light eats thereof, and in the love-desire brings itself into a holy being." ~ Jacob Boehme

Light and water are bodies
Foreign to one another.
They have nothing in common.
As we all do.
For nothing is all we have.
And it is precisely because
Of this that we acknowledge
The wondrous power of its presence.

At the river's edge I found a shell,
Campeloma parthenum,
The maiden river snail,
A vessel of emptiness filled
By the significance of language,
Its inhabitant *in absentia,*
No doubt transformed in the alembic
Of some newt's belly or sublimated
By the appetitive attentions
Of a dragonfly nymph.
I lifted it into the grey light
Of early morning when the air
Hung thick with the final shreds
Of mist risen from the shallows
And tried to look through it.
Though it glowed with borrowed
Light, my vision could not
Penetrate the virgin shell,

Nor could I inspect its folds
And secret recesses without destroying it.
Yet, I am assured of their existence,
And that they embrace nothing.

Salamanders

There is naturally in the human will
A real desire for a vision of God,
Independent of the vocation to
One's own supernatural destiny.
Or so writes a French theologian.
But, in all truth, he did not write these words.
At least not *these* words. He wrote his in French,
Of course, and I stole them still smoldering
From the cinders of an English translation.
But that's not true, either. I bent his words
To my own will, a very human one,
Perfecting them with subtleties of verse
And the capital's sublime agency.
But, see, even here I am playing games,
Avoiding the imperative question
Of whether or not we wish to see God.

Le sang de votre Sacré-Coeur m'a inondé a Montmartre—
The poet tells me. But for me it is the fire
That matters, the simultaneous destruction
And exaltation of the salamander in its own element
Until it separates into integral ash and smoke,
Evidence, if anything is, of the mystery of marriage.
The heart bleeds fire, and it is in this the poet drowns.
Shelley, his sodden *corpus* gifted to fire with red wine
And incense on the shore of the Tyrrhenian,
Would not yield his heart, for fire cannot consume fire.
The Beloved likewise gifts herself to sublimity.
Her heart burns and does not burn, exalted in fire,
For we see the holy face only in the ache and sacrifice of love.

Signs

"Magnas illas Dei litteras, quas Mundi machinae inscripsit."

We look everywhere for signs.
Evidence would be insufficient,
For it would only be a claim,
And to figure the Name
Within the sphere of rights
Would prove the greatest of blasphemies.

At the Shrine of Our Lady of Mariapoch,
In the middle of farmland in Burton, Ohio,
A bluebird nestles—and dies—
In the marble lap of Christ of the Deposition,
The rich blue strikingly pronounced
Before the Carrara marble's white ground.
Those afraid of death might read tragedy here
Along with the wholesale massacre
Of turtle eggs along the Florida shoreline
And the vanishing ice of the poles.
But they miss the disappearance of the sublime.

A girl sits in her car outside of the clinic
Filling out forms and weeping, as is her right;
On the otherwise immaculate sidewalk,
Sparrows argue over crusts of bread
While white jets strike whiter trails
Across the blue illumination of space:
Clear inscriptions in the greatest of letters
On the intricate machinery of the world.

13

Visions of Vladimir

Always it is the same. As Father Cyril
Whispers the secret words that shake the world
Free from the hypnosis of the Archons
And blesses the Kingdom with a song,
The Beautiful unfolding of itself,
Vladimir Solovyov wanders in and
Stands behind the altar, his hands in the
Pockets of his black frock coat or fumbling
With crumpled scraps of paper. Messages
From the Divine Sophia. Perhaps poetry.
Seeing me, he smiles and nods his head. His
Black eyes that sparkle like mica, his long
Black hair, paint him both eastern ascetic
And western bohemian. He has come
To assess my weekly progress in love.

Vladimir Sergeyevitch, you understand:
How love demands apostles, acolytes
Who hold candles before the holy face,
And that the only acceptable fuel
Is the self in its entirety,
The ecstasy and torment only signs,
Echoes of a more perfect love revealed
In colors and accidents of desire.

My Father: The Wind

On windy days like this
I remember my father,
How he sat in the backyard
At the rotting picnic table
Defying the wind,
Though black clouds swelled and pulsed
Like the alveoli of Hell.
The elms bent their mercurial frames
Before the absence of a greater god;
But he sat there, drinking Mohawk blue,
Muttering, "Take me. Take me, damn it,"
While my mother and siblings begged him
To take refuge in the basement.
They really wanted him to stay out there and die,
But felt obliged by blood and custom
To rise to the predictable drama of the moment.
At last, they retired to the dark of the cellar,
Nestled among mould-covered yukons
And the softening hides of onions,
To attend the small, static voice of a radio.
He killed his drink, banged the glass on rotten wood.
Lightning speared him through his lungs
And nailed me to his womb.

Everything you mother Buddha say

We feed through being,
Taking nourishment even through our eyes.
The goat   the wolf   the sphere
My mother cans tomatoes from our garden,
Bakes devil's food cakes from a mix.
Once she was angry with me
For piercing my ear with a ring.
When I locked myself in my room
To cry and burn the stars from my soul,
She knocked on my door with an axe.
Still, she called me to table, a dinner
Of boiled cabbage, potatoes whipped in milk.
We had milk with every meal
Goat's milk
Wolf's milk
The divine liquor called *lac virginis*
Bibite, fratres, et vivite!
If you get a bad mother,
You will become Sigmund Freud.
If you get the right mother,
You will become a poet.

It All Comes Down to Laundry

She certainly knew how to remove a stain from a sheet
Menstrual blood   semen   meconium   milk
The incontestable evidence of our impending death

> *in the river everything is green*
> *pale ropes of light hang from the surface*

In time, she could read a person's fortune from the stains
The marriage to a winged man
A journey by sea
The inevitable death by fire

> *your grandfather pulls you by the hair*
> *flops you on the creaking dock*
> *to draw the river from your breath*

She removed them through the most common of agencies
Vinegar, beer, sweat, and the incomparable solvent of her own tears.

The bedclothes, suspended from a silver cord,
Captured the terrible freshness of the wind
As if rising from the dead.

Camera Obscura

Claustrophobic quarters, where one window,
One aperture admits the world refuge.
Props are fashioned, employed or discarded,
Models adorned with this or another
Turban, this or another scarlet dress.

With shades projected in his frame like souls,
Vermeer explores the unconsidered lives
Of whores and drinkers, soldiers, pregnant girls,
Immortal in their failings like angels.

Woman's Work

in the Year of the Miraculous Child
  the elephant-headed god
accepted offerings of milk
  taking refreshment from a thimble
in his white marble form

my wife dreamt
  of a woman in blue
a shepherd of horses
  a valley of thunder & rivers

the pastel drawing of a black-haired woman
  and her newborn child stood
upside-down on the nightstand
  beside a vial of *oleum virginum*
and an antique looking-glass
  its birchwood frame carved in lilies

Pilcrow

¶

What is this golden coloring of the sky, in between the storms, as
swallows skim the pond's surface and green dragonflies light on
arrowheads and water lilies? The garden takes on a glow, a mantle of
phosphorescence, and I hear the thrumming I sometimes find in sleep.
Certainly a goddess.

¶

The birds were drunk. Fallen mulberries had fermented from wind-
born yeast. The birds chattered and madly flapped their wings until,
exhausted, they collapsed. We picked them up. They were starlings
and grackles, warm in our hands. We hid them underneath the
spruces, but in the morning found nothing but feathers, a few bones.

¶

Melissa asks me what color occurs most often in my dreams. Strangely,
I don't know. She asks me this in a dream, of course, and I am angry
with myself that I can't say, even though I look around. Is there even
color? *Est et non.* Descartes looked to dreams to confirm his
materialism. We look to materialism to confirm our dreams. *Non et est.*
Is this not the only dialectic?

¶

Bibliomancy. *What can I do to gather up and answer that universal and
enveloping embrace? Quomodo comprehendam ut comprehensus sum?* The
Holy Spirit lurks in every book, every line, between all letters. In the
stain of ink and in the pure emptiness of paper. He defies rhetoric,
intention, expectation. He writes within writing. Behind writing.
Subtext. Context. *Textus.* Something woven. It's not that there is no
such thing as an author. It's that there is only the one. We really are not
our own. Plotinus says it best: *Things here are signs.*

The Garden of the Philosopher

These bastard orioles have stolen all my fruit:
Green medlars and quince, green Cox's Orange Pippins.
I will wait in ambush, hidden in a spruce thicket.
A bottle of ouzo. A BB gun.

The hummingbird buzzes outside my bedroom window,
Thrusting his slender proboscis into the lavender bells of the hosta.
The symbolism is obvious. The sentiment laudable.

We buried the placenta under a Rose of Sharon in Ferndale, Michigan
Where we saw the Virgin Mary in a cloud of white herons on a day I
avoided suicide.

In the dream, St. Augustine tells me to save the half-dead oak tree.
He doesn't care about cost or how pointless the endeavor.
I hold in my hands a rusty bow saw, a dead sparrow.

Death of the Hermaphrodite

We weren't surprised when we learned
    About the Hermaphrodite's suicide.
Found in a crowded attic at thirty-five
    Above a bar in Hamtramck, Michigan,
It was another tragic victim of a combined overdose
    Of generic Viagra and strychnine-spiked merlot.

We'd helped it through its bouts of melancholia:
    The failed stabs at being husband, at being wife;
The impulsive, though ardent, experiments
    With the religious right and the political left;
The failed careers as commodities broker and doula.

We were hopeful when the great Michel Foucault
    Spoke out in its defense—
Writing papers, giving symposia—
    But to what end?
Soon he abandoned himself to the bathhouses
    And the politics of his own despair.

In the end, the Hermaphrodite wanted
    The same things we all want:
The assurances of love,
    The acknowledgment of being,
Nice messages on the voice mail,
    A pronoun we can live with.

Blood and Water, Smoke and Light

I. Elements

We found him on the shore of Livorno,
An angelic face bloated with sea water,
Brine crystals crusting his lashes with stars.
In the right-hand pocket of his jacket,
Hid Sophocles' *Trichiniae* in Greek,
And in the left a new volume of Keats.
I drew my thumbnail across the leather,
And instantly the trail filled with water.

The Carabinieri feared cholera,
Denied passage for Roman burial.
We begged to burn the corpse upon the strand,
And lent the pyre *vin santo*, myrrh, and oil,
Commending his soul to the *Eumenides*.
Five hours we watched and waited for the fire
To reduce his remains to ash and smoke.
But when, finally, the chest broke open,
The ribs spreading as if fingers released,
Or as if we ourselves had grown smaller,
We saw, revealed in blood and fire and light,
The apotheosis of poetry.

II. *Parrhesia*

It is a problem,
This abandonment,
Sublimity of pleasures,
In which one not only

Enters other selves
But loses oneself entire.
Nothing stirs.

Nothing speaks.
Nothing, indeed, is.
N'cest pas?
Behold the ultimate *expérience limite.*
What an extreme honor it is
To have been infected with you,
Delimited by the politics of desire.
Farewell.

III. The Secrets of Corrosives

In the taxonomy of feathers,
The soul is often omitted.
But it is there, subtle
In the calamus.
A substance of interest only
To children and poets.

I once saw him sweep a goose feather
Across the blackened face of his copperplate.
The tiny bubbles ascended
Through acid water from scratches
And crosshatchings,
And he laughed like a child
At the transmutation of so many devils.

This morning his face was leaden,
The full pale skin thinly veiling his skull,
As he lay oppressed with life and breath.

When he opened his eyes,
Filmed and glazed with rheum,
He told us of angels and apples,
And of the delights in pure desire.
He slept again, and we watched.

At eventide, the August sun entered the room.
Awakened by the light, he sat upright,
Opened once again his eyes to weep,
His countenance become fresh and fair,
And he chaunted of the coloured glories
Beheld in heaven in a voice full of bells.
And so he left us.

IV. Whispers

On an index card he scribbled,
"Quelquefois je me déteste,"
In lead pencil according to the testimony
Of the always reliable Nurse Causeur.
A missive to accompany
His violation of the rose.
At which he smirked in his bed.
In which again rose his volition.

The doctors said his arteries were iron,
And they labored to admit
The accustomed needle.
He blamed his seventy asthmatic years
And the polluted stink of inferior breaths.
Others named his various addictions,
And his particular obsession with the will.

Mucus rattled in his chest.
He fumbled with the lamp,
Then motioned for his pipe.
We brought it and the matches,
Though he no longer knew us.
We thought it a performance
Another of his absurdities.
But he was in earnest.

Long he looked from the matches
Spilled on the coverlet,
To the brass lamp on the stand,
To the pipe he explored with tremulous
Digits, as if a moment of discovery.
He rasped, "I am perplexed,"
In a voice thin as paper,
And then, as if by magic, disappeared.

V. An Epistle of Comfort

The breath of the black horses formed in clouds.
They snorted, stamped, and shook their charcoaled manes,
Acknowledging the humour of the hour
With a resignation similar to men's.
Behind them in the cart, hung in reverse,
The black robin swung, his face covered with earth.

They cut him down, then set him on his feet,
And rolled his carriage under the scaffold.
Though drawn, he smiled upon the crowd to see
So many goodly creatures assembled
And gave his chaplet to a little child,
Who shivered in the February cold.

"*In manus tuas*" he began his prayer,
And, slow and grave, the cart was drawn away.
He just as slowly rose into the air,
While we avoided one another's gaze.
And when the hangman lifted up his head,
None cried, Traitor, though many cried for blood.

Self-portrait with Graveyard

I draw tire treads over immaculate snow,
Sip yesterday's coffee from a travel mug.
Crows perch on headstones and crosses,
And I note the names meticulously engraved
Over the ominous doors of mausoleums:
Dodge. Hudson. Grinnel. Martin.
The sun shines, sparkles on snow.
Granite monuments and the contorted
Branches of hawthorn trees glisten with new ice,
While bronze yews and arborvitae no
Longer deserve the distinction evergreen.
I dreamt this morning.
In the dream I follow the tracks of a deer
Over the gray snow of my backyard.
Obviously a tremendous buck:
Two marks embellish the heart-
Shaped hoofprints like eyes.
I look in the garage for a weapon,
But find my friend, Emmanuel,
Who hands me a gift, a box
Wrapped in paper.
The package says *I am.*
I wheel through immaculate snow.
On the black marble stairs of a neoclassical
Tomb a copper goddess mourns the dead.
A red-tailed hawk rises from the ground,
Pinions of white velvet.

Meditations in Times of Wonder

Orchestra Hall in nineteen eighty-five:
A concert of John Cage's latest works,
The auditorium populated
With art students and intellectuals—
One hundred-twenty people in a three-
Thousand seat room. By the second tonal
Experiment half of the patrons slept.
The auteur sat rigid in his ornate
Box clutching the armrests, ready to jump.

.

The Waldorf School in Indian Village
On a cold Sunday evening in April:
A troupe of local Anthroposophists
Performed in Goethe's Green Snake fairytale,
A play of alchemy and miracles.
The players moved and spoke like ancient ghosts,
Forgoing graces of human gesture
And of the language common to the damned.
Homunculi captured on a scaffold,
Sexless, distant, prematurely embalmed.

.

My grandfather, Michael Patrick Conlon,
Born in Carrick-on-Shannon, Ireland, and
For the last half-century of Detroit,
Strains to sit up in his hospital bed.
Cancer has collapsed the great, barreled chest,
Radiation loosened the once ruddy
Skin that covers his skull like a soft veil.
He tells me of the music he's made, the

Women he's made love to, the sins he's tried.
He tells me of the ghosts that visit his
Bedside in the milky hours when no one
Else is there: His brother John whose bones rest
In St. Mary's churchyard, County Leitrim,
A boy whose sorrowful shroud he's carried
Across the ocean and sixty-three years;
His sister Mae who died a fortnight past
And told him of her death. They speak of home.

·

I'm in the garden of Christ Church, Cranbrook,
Parish of artists and auto barons.
The wind tumbles a Burger King wrapper
Across the tidy, empty parking lot.
Spruce trees drop brown needles and green, sticky
Cones on immaculate lawns and pathways.
In a schoolyard nearby a man pushes
His son on a swing hung with rusty chains
That creak with each pull of the child's weight.
A crow screams curses from the belfry's crown.
But I am in the garden of this church
And see Jesus crucified in a rose.

·

William Butler Yeats, I sit here enchained
To the oak spindles of this rocking chair
While you tear the liver of my spirit.
I have rejected much that you stand for,
Though in my youth my ways were much as yours.
Only imagination's primacy,
History's incarnation of aeons,
And the holiness of biography
Have I held on to. But these are enough.

The Dead

I.

A graveyard in my childhood was a place for games.
A place where boys and girls gathered at dusk to hide
And seek behind mausoleums and monuments,
Under bushes and in the branches of white pines.
The atmosphere of death and mysteries of graves
Gave our games an excitement, an anxiety
Even, as we explored our genius for a deep
Human capacity to imagine evil.
The groundskeeper stumbled upon us as we played,
But in our state we thought it was an angry ghost
Who chased us over graves and crumbling pavement.
We jumped the iron fence and tore our clothes or worse,
Our skin, on the menacing teeth of the pickets.
My brother John opened his knee as he jumped down.
We washed away the streaming blood and saw the white
Gristle, the pink meat of his flesh, black flecks of iron.

II.

After the football game we parked beneath the willows at Old Redford
Cemetery. It was a safe place to party, out of the concerns of the police
and beyond the hearing of nosy neighbors. Kidneys bursting with
Stroh's, the boys pissed against headstones. We swung from the arms
of marble crosses and sat cavalier on monuments like gods. The girls
huddled in a circle close to the trees. They laughed about stupid boys
and flicked ashes from their menthol cigarettes. They wrapped close
their short jackets, protecting themselves from the October wind
and other cold pleasures. But one girl sat in a car and cried: Carol
Angellini, who'd buried her mom in the spring. Both lay beyond our
consideration, immortal as we were.

III.

I made it to Lisa's graveside
twenty years after the funeral
I did not chance to attend,
following a day of landscaping,
more gravedigger than grave.
Two decades of guilt and avoidance
had dulled the face of the headstone
and its chiseled Roman script.
Exhausted from wrestling trees,
I slept there until friends arrived:
Ken, Danny and Lou
(whose son Ted sleeps nearby –
patron saint of fallen wires).
Then Terry, Julie and Sara came,
the dearly beloved
brother, sister-in-law and niece
of a girl who'd slept her
death in a running car.
We arranged ourselves
in a circle, an ellipse really,
around her silent hill;
improvised a make-shift requiem
characterized by guitar mass psalms,
modern poetry
and unfamiliar prayers.
Sticks of incense
thrust from the ground
like burning flowers.
The angel of death
did not free us from our shame,
but allowed us to return,
each to his difficult life.

Him to the Night

"Abwärts wend ich mich zu der heiligen, unaussprechlichen, geheimnisvollen Nacht."

1. All things here are monsters. We hold to what we think to be lovely—a pale pink quince blossom, the sound of a mandolin, the smell of freshly-turned soil, even the beloved—but, in time, they all lose their splendor. The light which emanated from them slips away. To where? What is this quality that unfolds only when it unfolds and fools us into looking for it everywhere? Where does it reside?

2. In the night we deliver our prayers to the darkness, hoping there is relief from despair. Even those who believe they have transcended belief. This is truly something holy, unspoken, and mysterious.

3. The blue of the sky is an illusion, the color of darkness illuminated by earthshine. If we could reach our hands beyond it and into the darkness, would we? None of us is entitled to the kiss. Clouds break before the waning crescent moon, the horns pointing back to where so much lies hidden.

4. Light poured into her from the Divine Sophia so much so that she was filled and became invisible. Ever after, he looked for her in the stars, when the dark of the *Ungrund* was closest to revealing her. Then, one day in March, *Verkündigung*, he at last surrendered himself to her splendor.

Icon Writing

"We stand all in God's field, and we grow to God's glory, and to his works of wonder."

We burned the leaves before the storm arrived:
Sweet-smelling maple, leathery oak, crisp poplar and apple,
Then added black walnuts in their darkening hulls, dry fir cones.
The clouds hung low and grey—we could smell the rain—
And the smoke brought water to our eyes.
The next morning, flame still sputtered
Beneath a damp mound of ash
Like a pudding or a cooling meteor.
After three days the fire extinguished itself
And we bore the cold remnants to the garden,
Now a network of compost piles.
We sprinkled the charcoal and ash in layers,
Straw from the goat shed, filings of zinc and copper,
Egg shells, faded stalks of parsley, raw sugar and sea salt,
Wine lees, bones, and bedding from the hens, then
Covered all with soil we broke free from a crust of frost:
Our only contribution to the economy of grace.

Anatomy of Nature

Something in analysis speaks directly of death,
The human comedy of making inferences
About what lives by examining what does not.
In this spirit, natural philosophy changed
Its name to science, love gave way to knowledge,
And perception began to check itself with theory.
An impoverished set of tools.

So we persist in our obsession with the *Organon*,
Even after seventeen hundred years of spectacular
Failures, though we still cannot dissect light, nor
Find the soul, nor explain why water, nature's
Nonconformist, flouts the laws of physics, expanding
When it should contract, contracting when
All else expands. We continue cutting away at the world,
Beloved, as if our violence could establish the city
We so hope to praise, as if the heavens declared no glory,
As if light and water were not the greatest of metaphors.

Koinonia

Saints look upon me from the wall over my desk
A faded holy card of Our Lady of Guadalupe
Robert Southwell and John Donne
Guillaume Apollinaire
And a haunting almost *sfumato* black and white image
Of St. Teresia Benedicta of the Cross I printed from the internet
My pigtailed daughter Zelie playing the violin
My brown-eyed daughter Isabel wearing wings and holding a star
My dark son Aidan wearing a red baseball uniform and holding a red
    baseball bat
A *retablo* of the Holy Child of Atocha
A cross made of nails
Encrusted with tiger eyes and turquoise
A keychain without a key
And a color print of the Sacred Heart
With holes in the background that look like stars
Stars in the background that look like holes

You who look upon me through all of these
And who sprinkled wisdom throughout the universe
You who inscribed the first poem and opened the darkness
Who brings forth bread from the earth
Who created the fruit of the vine
And mixed shadow with light, giving us color
That we might find a way to rejoice
Repair what we have broken
The nature and design of ourselves
That we may be awakened to the music of the kiss
And discern the secret of your warmth
So we can know for certain that all space is alive
With the laughter you uttered at the first shining

Catholic Devotional Poem with Double-Barrel Twelve-Gauge

Sometimes the woods seem so dead,
Especially after all the leaves have fallen
And the sun hides behind the covering clouds.
No wind, no movement of animals,
Even the crows are silent.
Then the twelve-gauge feels colder, heavier,
A burden claiming more than weight.
On such a day I reached deep into the woods.

After getting lost in a copse,
A messy tangle of jack pine and Virginia creeper,
I broke into a patch of stag-horn sumac.
Stands of pin oak and hickory on three sides,
Scrub junipers and dead bracken.
Looking for rabbits, I stumbled over the stone
Outline of a house long-since vanished,
The chimney now a pile of rubble.
I unearthed an iron ring on a spike
And a triangle of blue and white porcelain,
Wiped off the dirt and placed them on a stone.

About twenty feet from the house
(That was not a house)
I found a forgotten domestic shrine
Covered with lichen and moss,
But remarkably intact. Obscured
By sumac and the branches
Of a recently fallen oak,
The shrine was designed as a grotto,
Fieldstone held together with mortar,

Now cracked across the top
Where a limb must have struck.

In an attitude of blessing and concern,
A concrete casting of the Virgin stood
On an outcropping of stone.
Dew dappled the face and veil,
And only a few patches of faded blue paint
Remained on the covering mantle.
I looked into her eyes and offered a prayer,
A chiastic breathing of hope and grace,
And the voice of a sparrow broke into my reverie,
Or perhaps my reverie became a voice.
On the ledge before the Virgin lay
A handful of coins, pinecones and acorns,
A crow's feather, the shell of a snail,
And the delicate remains of a snakeskin.

Reading Boehme
on the Darkest Day of the Year

What is it that causes a flock of starlings, all at once,
To wheel, turn, or tumble in the magnificent breathing
Of their migration, rising from bare oak trees, swamp maples,
And alders, from telephone wires and cracked asphalt,
Falling onto withered meadows, dry bean fields, and housetops,
Their voices filling the horizon with fire?

Three days of rain: a constant drizzle punctuated with the occasional
Deluge melted the ten inches of snow that fell five days before.
The grass, out of sight for such a short time, had
Lost its weak green and turned a putrid shade of amber. All this,
Against the grey of the day, suggested I look for other signatures.
The pond reflected only darkness, and a grey heron—
Apparently not interested in migration—
Walked upon its black surface like an illusionist.

I read somewhere that the universe is a hologram,
A dynamic representation of movement and flux,
A part disclosing the whole, the whole ensouling each part.
Cars rattle down our muddy road, headlights unable to penetrate
The fog and drizzle, appearing and disappearing with all the poverty
Of imagination. The hens no longer lay, mice nibble at russets in the
    cellar,
And we count the dwindling pennies in the bank.

I know this poem's supposed to be about Boehme, but I can't focus
My attention on his text. I can't tear my gaze from its obsession
With all that is broken, all that is grey and dying in the reality of
    appearances,

With all that is hidden or disclosed in the dark tensions between love
  and anger.
I crouched near the hive and placed my ear to the wood:
The thrum of bees in their vocation, generating warmth to preserve
  the queen.
We search through the greyness for the kiss,
For the place where bread and wine are no longer bread and wine,
For a place to place the weakness of our inconsequential gifts,
And deliver ourselves to the consequences of ultimate humility,
The part disclosing the whole, and the whole ensouling each part.

A pond . . . a lake . . . a river

The Auvergne . . . a pond in January where I broke through the ice and tasted water for the first time . . . struck by Apollo . . . arrived in rags . . . my pockets full of bread and poems, my head full of stars and gods . . . the mournful, lonely earth, the shepherds . . . the breezes rise . . . all, all so lovely . . . the burning forests . . . the death of Hector

A body of water . . . a body . . . water . . . exhausted by poverty, fished all night . . . prayed for success, not out of envy (so I told myself) but out of, I said, care . . . the storm . . . a dream of walking . . . the impossibility of kindness . . . my own habitual failures . . . a body

The river speaks its own dialect, a language opened only to silence . . . in stillness it reflects even the faintest stars, asserts its nature in movement when all else disappears . . . the washed bed of pebbles . . . the soft bend of the bank . . . the hypnotic charm of the current . . . the poet steps into a river like a priest . . . cupped hands holding water . . . swallows skim along the surface . . . the swaying of trees . . . fallen leaves . . . wind brushing the face of the river . . . the river

Thomas Traherne

I see him, as if in a parallel universe,
   Writing verses on a slate.
The long brown hair, the Anglican collar,
   The eye familiar with the splendor of God,
   The face that could never be old.
He writes in earnest and the chalk
   Scratches and squeaks on the stone,
   Coughing and singing its voluntary end.
He laughs like a child as he takes up
   A sponge to wipe the black field clean,
   Filling the emptiness with poetry,
Then wrings it with a joyous gushing of rain
   Into a bowl flashing with words and wonder.

Martyrology

"Spectaculum facti sumus Deo, angelis et hominibus."

1.
Children sprinkled by martyr's blood at Tyburn,
Mothers begging the action of grace.
A young lawyer watches Southwell die, remembers
Campion and his own mother's words:
Though these things be far from thine eye,
They shall ever be present unto your memory.

2.
Presence to the text discloses another presence:
Parousia shimmering beyond the contours of narratology,
Hidden in the syllogism, seeded in the poetic.
The text becomes the rumble of a train, the sacrifice
Of a rose, angels rising from smokestacks
Spiraling and weeping in their ascent.

3.
Mostly it is seen in the blue of the stars and in the Virgin's eyes, for
Everything is this: the appearance of the beautiful, a kind of radiance.
The blue of the winter sky over Toksovo when the prisoners
Defied the guards and prayed . . . the blue of his eyes like shards of
    Armenian
Ice . . . the blue of the bullet that opened his skull and filled his body
    with light.

Martyrdom

"Ἐγὼ γὰρ ἤδη σπένδομαι."

it always comes down to sacrifice
self-identity over political charade
a moment of metaphysical anagnorisis
and a lack of will to persist in appearances
resulting in the appropriate level of dramaturgy
the blood and pathos
the usual speech from the scaffold
the testament etched in burned brick with a nail

all this I would prefer to avoid
but my martyrdom has already begun
as has yours, gentle reader
mine by writing them
yours by reading these words
though most of all in the bothersome thoughts
that stand in defiance of the archons
who trouble the wind and waves with fear
and pretend they hold the rights to language

the day eventually comes
you recognize who you are
and who the being beyond being is
that love is a chemical regeneration of the flesh
flesh in so much pain it burns at his embrace
wants nothing more than to see him suffer
in the name of some common good
and then it all comes down to sacrifice

Angel

in word, gesture, stillness . . . in movement over water . . . as shepherd
of bees . . . as awakening in seeds . . . poetry . . . the music in dreams,
an augmented ninth chord sustained from everlasting . . . I was
baptized at Pentecost in the parish church of St Cecelia, Livernois,
in the City of Death . . . at age three I fell off a pier into the river . . .
greenness, trails of light from the surface, shimmering . . . my
grandfather grabbed me by the hair as I bobbed up . . . no one had
noticed . . . everything since has been gift

Ode to Postmodern Catholic Apologists

"Seul en Europe tu n'es pas antique ô Christianisme"
~ Guillaume Apollinaire

Enough on Tolkien and Lewis,
Enough images from the Renaissance,
Enough Tridentine nostalgia.
Enough neo-Neo-Scholasticism
And pious Romanticism.
I do not trust an ethos of retrieval.
We need new forms, brothers and sisters,
New ways to show how culture is made ever new
From the most authentic of sources.
Show me how the Church is relevant in the present,
Not what is significant about the past.
Show me how Christ breathes life
Into the wheel of the year
And the works of human hands,
How his beauty inheres the universe,
How Wisdom fills all space
And how the Spirit dissolves time
Through the kairotic disruption of the now.
Let all else die.
For we live by resurrection.

The Blood

Blood, the real
blood: this
might be worth showing up for.

~*Fran*ʒ *Wright*

I. *"In the running waters"*

seventeen below last night, Feast of Theophany
coldest temperatures in my lifetime
we slept in our clothes

the goat had squirmed out of her sweater and stood in the shed
shivering and pathetic this morning when I brought her a bucket of
warm water to drink and a cup of grain sweetened by molasses

found one of the hens, a blue egg laying Ameraucana, dead in a nesting
  box
threw her on a snowbank, waiting on coyotes or a thaw, whichever
  comes first

prayed the bees survived, set candles on the hives and sprinkled them
with holy water
which turned in midair to droplets of ice

II. *Smyrna, the Aegean*

Seventy years ago today my priest, then a boy of seven, found his
grandfather, also a priest, in church after the Turks had savaged their
village. The night before, the careful father hid all of the women of the
family—infants and girls, maidens and mothers—in a hole in the

kitchen floor and covered it with a greasy board. Then he went into the church to pray before the icon of the Virgin. In the morning he hung from the iconostasis by a lasso.

III. *Poiesis*

The blood is real, Franz.
The blood is real.

Ode to George Herbert

What act is more emblematic of hubris than writing a religious poem?
You knew this, gentle, reverend Herbert, drawing us to your raw
    anxieties
In meditation on the holy river: the inevitable conclusion
That all our works are vanity.
                                        All my lines are tainted with the stain and
    fragrance
Of sin. As with all forms of making, poetry is evidence of lack and failure,
Disclosing the desire of the poet for completion and a thin posterity,
Praising the made, forgetting the Maker—as you confessed in hesitant
    whispers.
Freud would blame the id, of course, finding reason in urges, drives,
And the primitive, though I locate the root in a more traditional culprit:
I have met him (this is no metaphor) and he visits me whenever I'm weak.
But this is no excuse. My sins remain *my* sins, my failures as a man
    reflected
In lines I write in hope of apostolic benediction or for that moment
When heaven opens and the angel of poetry risks its terrible descent,
Though I persist in artifice, crafting broken verse with a meagre set of
    tools,
Playing the part of the religious poet. In one of your poems, this is the line
Where God rescues the speaker from despair. But I resist this desired
    temptation.
I will hazard an end in my own voice.
                                        In face of the impossibility
Of the possible, I confess it not my doing but that articulations
Of grace fill both the world and words with movement, turning red blood
    and black ink to light
In ways I will never be able to discern. For he hides in everything, even
    sin.

The Phenomenology of Phenomenology
(before an image of St. Teresia Benedicta of the Cross)

presence unfolds presence . . . paper dissolves in smoke . . .
reappearance . . . something that is not paper, not ink, not . . .
ist . . . eyes flash and recede, the darkened mouth . . . remembrance
of candles . . . fire . . . the feeling, the reality, of love sensed,
tasted . . . more than philosophy . . . a deeper presence . . . horizon
. . . another horizon . . . *ist*

Nomina

then all things were only names
forcing us to grow clever in augmentation
and in the hermeneutics of extrapolation
the trim and glitter of a mediated world
where the lanterns illuminate
the holy image only with our shadows
that we might more conveniently praise
at a price we can afford

Martyrdom (2)

"If you follow Jesus and don't end up dead, it appears you have some explaining to do." ~ Terry Eagleton

to dwell in words
dwell in truth
in blood
this is already martyrdom
the kairotic moment
when the universe opens
and the real fills all things
with blood
with truth
with words

Viriditas

Light comes earlier in the morning, softening
The darkened house before the children awake.
And I wonder when the frogs will return, invisible,
Though their voices trill joyfully from bare trees, from half-frozen
    ponds
And marshes in correspondence to the rise and fall of the temperature,
An annunciation of the greening of all things, of absence and return.

One March temperatures reached into the eighties for two weeks.
Turtles roused early from their muddy beds under the water
And apple trees began to bud weeks ahead of schedule.
We spent evenings on the porch sipping wine, eating bread and olives
    by candlelight,
Celebrating the return of the warmth and a respite from heating bills.
But then things turned cold again, as we knew they would. Frost
Killed the apple blossoms and with them our hopes of harvest.
My daughter found five dead turtles in the thin ice at the edge of the
    pond
And ran to me in a panic, wondering if there was something I could do.
I can still see one of them, a big Blanding's, the legs and neck flaccid,
    head
Gently swinging as I lifted it from the water. I remember
The pale yellow streak along the throat and a ring of ice stuck to the
    shell,
The small eyes closed in a signature of primordial acquiescence.

The Wilderness

After a week I forgot about the cold,
And sometime later—a month?—
I first saw the colors:
The tones and subtleties of the flowers
And grasses shining through the browns,
The bleached-out yellows and faded greens
Of their dead winter forms.
Though not like echoes.
More as harbingers, rather,
Or perhaps something more permanent.
Something of promise. Even here.
At night, if it was clear,
I could look past the branches of the trees
To the stars and, on occasion,
Trace the motions of the planets or
See the aurora pulsing magenta,
Emerald and white on the northern
Horizon. When the moon was strong
It kept me from sleep,
So I prayed.
In spring there were salamanders,
Fiddleheads and mushrooms.
The voices of frogs surrounded me,
Shimmering in the air, only quiet
When it grew too cold to sing.
The floor of the forest turned green
And white with trillium and mayapple
Pushing through the leaf mold
And then the fields opened their colors,

Calling the butterflies and birds.
And everywhere there were bees.
At last, one day in summer,
Looking for a deeper solitude,
I discovered the river. Light
Sparkled on its surface, even at night,
As if it came from within the water.
But that would be impossible.
I awaited his arrival.

Mysterion

The congregation waits for the procession to begin. My pale green dalmatic rustles in answer to the wind and I see my son Aidan buttoning his cassock. Why aren't you ready? I ask him. A little girl with hair the color of coal holds an icon without an image. Lifting the golden book of the Gospels, Fr. Cyril says it's time to begin, but I ask him to wait. Vines grow from the border of his phelonion and wreathe about his neck. I rip them out, but they grow back.

This happened in a dream,
Of course, a dream of Pentecost.
I will not risk explication,
Brothers and sisters,
For the dream, like the poem,
(If an angel-born dream,
If a poem from the *Poietes*)
Only suffers under such scrutiny,
Until it at last becomes but a corpse,
The source of its life fled,
The *mysterion* present only to conjecture.

Adoration

The image of a mother, draped in deep green velvet
Like the color of the sea at morning
Faces of infants billow in clouds and she presents to you,
In the way of a gift, the wonderful child

Balsam trees sway in the wind and on the pond's surface
Which trembles from movements of the fish below
The sun touches the horizon and opens its warmth
Turning the snow over the meadows all blue
And a voice calls from beyond the ink's impression and its ground,
Shimmers and fades in response to your attention

Something comes to you, a shrine of sorts, though
Dependent on the interplay of shadow and light,
The gentle, unobtrusive birth of color

And the gaze…*what is it?* the real?
How often you have felt its warmth
Without returning even the courtesy of a smile
But instead felt terror, rather, or something like terror
And looked away, ashamed at your own disclosure

Time, another kind of time, Kecharitomene,

The Desert

"More than we fear, we love the holy desert."
~ *Thomas Merton*

The question of fecundity,
For all is desert.
The question of sterility.
For all is desert.
We are not victims of time
And at the mercy of the rains.
Though we are clearly victims of time
And at the mercy of the rains.
A time of victims.
Threats are inscribed (by whom?) in the spiny skins
Of succulents and in the rough hides of lizards.
(We roasted three of them over a fire made of dead grass
And, after devouring them, they made us thirsty.)
Dust devils and the oppression of the sun.
The harsh blue of the sky
And the quivering of the air.
The sparkling stars.
Prayer, an economy of shade and shadow.
The crescent moon, thin and pale-yellow,
Setting at the purpled horizon.
The mercy of the rains and time.
The god of the desert.
The voices that come with sleep.
The holiness.

The Liturgy of Hours

For S. C.

Concern melts away in prayer, in liturgy. Λειτουργός. An echo. *Hard
is the work of the Lord.* The words of a dying philosopher, a dying poet,
a man dissolved beyond our seeing. Herbert, Traherne, Apollinaire,
Novalis . . . all gone by forty, their suffering joining frailty to the
tremulous light. In much the same way, my friend now vanishes before
me, a kind of counter-kairos by which *he* becomes present to God,
though the procession itself is far from pleasant. The concern again.
Sacrifice, a kind of singing.

Aubade

This morning my daughter
Zelie sits writing a book,
The Box of Poems, the story
Of an impoverished family
Who discover a book interred
In the belly of an ancient trunk.
Words full of pathos and God,
Of salmon and rivers and stars.
The find brings them wealth
And, with it, the ability to send
Their crippled child, a black-haired
Boy named Danny Willy,
To hospital in Dublin,
The poetic center of the world.

I button my grey wool coat,
Arrange my long white scarf,
Then kiss Zelie on the head.
Isabel gives me a hug,
Baby Daniel offers a kiss,
Though, at the moment,
With his oatmeal still on the stove,
Brother Gabriel is not interested
In dispensing affection.
I hug my wife and she whispers
The familiar words, "We're out of money.
Use the credit card if you need gas."

In my pickup truck the color of cornflowers
I find a pen, its blue ink cold and slow,
And try to write a poem on the back of a receipt.
The sun sparkles on the frosted windshield,
The awakened universe spiraling, spiraling.

The Gnostic Gospels for Idiots

As the story goes, somewhere in the desert of Wadi, a group of disaffected monks with Liberal Arts degrees, but an immense distaste for literature, recorded their nightmares and preserved them in jars. Probably Mason jars. They were intellectuals. Like those guys wearing Hawaiian shirts behind the counter at Dave's Comix, or those artist-types with the really cool haircuts who work at video stores and like to talk about Jarmusch's *oeuvre* but roll their eyes anytime anybody asks for *The Sound of Music*. This is all pertinent because, basically, the Gnostic scriptures *are* Coptic comic books, texts peopled by denizens of other worlds: beings with superhuman powers, bearing outlandish names, bent on battling evil geniuses in order to reveal the conspiracy that *is* is. And love? Forget love. This stuff is for people who want to *know*. (Hence its appeal for academics.) But, wait! If the Gnostic gospels are comic books, then wouldn't that make comics *midrash*? Which, in turn, would make graphic novels (from Gr. *graphein*, "writing," and Lt. *novum*, "new") mystical-philosophical tractates designed to awaken sleeping humanity to the reality behind creation's degraded veil. Neotech hieroglyphics! Hold it! Stan Lee, founder of superhero conglomerate Marvel Comics (from Lt. *mirari*, "to wonder at"), even calls his readers "true believers"! On the Web, graphic novel wunderkind Neil Gaiman examines *What It Takes to Be a God*—just like it says in *The Apocryphon of John*: "Man came forth because of the shadow of the light which is in him. And his thinking was superior to all those who had made him." This is cutting edge theology. Yet so simple.

Cento: Light and blood are one and the same thing

The afterimage of a flying lion
Metaphor and thaumaturgy
Three days without washing
Slept on the ground
Vanished, became volatile
Then walked out once more
Beneath the laughing stars

Agon

The starling we found,
Headless, really only wings,
Food for an owl or crow.

From the train I see a small Anglican church a quarter mile away,
Its churchyard surrounded in the traditional habit of graves.
The life-size crucifix appears at this distance disturbingly real.
A tractor tears lines across a field. Clouds of dust and seagulls.

After a meal of bullfrog the blue racer suns himself near his burrow.
I set the muzzle of my twelve-gauge on his head
And he wraps his cerulean torso along the length of the barrel.
I lift him into the wind, the apotheosis of my self.

Jesus. Movies.

1.

When I was a twelve
Channel 7's Four O'Clock Movie
Played *King of Kings* with Jeffrey Hunter
In two parts, Holy Monday and Maundy Thursday.
Spots for Anacin and Levi's interspersed the parables.
The Crucifixion, interrupted by a State Farm commercial:
Didn't expect the unexpected?
I found a paintbrush and some leftover paints
From an old paint-by-number set,
Dusted off a remnant piece of paneling,
And painted the Crucifixion in fire.
In my awkwardness I gave
Jesus tremendous arms.
He was a kindly gorilla,
A "T" in imperfect lower-case,
An exploding airplane.

2.

My friend, Brian, is annoyed at a movie,
The Last Temptation of Christ.
He doesn't like the way Jesus reaches
Into his chest, yanks out his heart,
And shows the astounded disciples
His pulsing, slimy organ.
It's not in the book.

Maybe it's all over the book.

3.

I am watching Franco Zeffirelli's
Jesus of Nazareth on VHS.
The blurb on the box assures me this is

A Film Conceived, Planned and Made With Love

(Color, 1976)
Maintaining the perfect balance between
religious fervor and realism...

My son, Tommy, runs to me in a panic saying,
"Those people who want you to go to another church are here!"
I pause the video as blue-eyed Jesus,
His arm upraised in a gesture of authority,
Stands before the tomb of Lazarus.
Looking out through the curtains
I see a troop of Jehovah's Witnesses
Bailing out of a minivan, one by one,
The men in navy blue business suits and power ties,
The women in broad-brimmed hats and conservative
Print dresses with large, floppy collars.
They walk door to door,
Hawking copies of *The Watchtower* and *Awake!*
Ringing doorbells, smiling.
Jesus flickers, shimmers on the screen,
His arm still uplifted,
Lazarus still uncalled.

4.

This is a movie.
This is a Super 8 movie
Of my sister Carrie's First Communion.
The altar boy trying to get his cowlick

To stay down is me.
Spit, wipe.
Spit, wipe.
Carrie wears white shoes, white tights,
A little white dress with faux-pearl frogs,
A white veil garnished with the same plastic pearls,
And darling little white gloves.
I am dressed differently:
Black cassock,
White surplice.
At the end of Mass
The little communicants
File out of church two by two,
As if emerging from the ark
Or the assembly line.
Fade.

Here we are in front of the church,
Before the white marble statue of the Virgin.
Carrie is smiling.
I am smiling.
Mom and Dad are smiling.
Everyone's smiling.
Little girls in white dresses and veils,
Little boys in dark trousers,
Light blue long-sleeve shirts
And clip-on ties wait their turn
To take pictures with Fr. Ryan.
The wind musses hair, disturbs veils.
In the distance cars process and stop,
Process and stop, in the peristalsis of traffic.
The film darkens, splinters,
Explodes in white light.

Absence/Presence

1.

The young man sees the three drops of blood from a wounded goose blended with snow and dissolves in reverie. It reminds him of the complexion of his beloved. In the words of the poet, "He became lost in contemplation." The splendor of the beloved shines through the fabric of the world, the immaterial image of the material disclosing its absolute necessity. The rupture of blood on snow. The sacred. The flesh.

2.

A naturalized French citizen and a Jew, he spent much of World War II interred in a German prison camp while his wife and daughter were hidden in a monastery. Meanwhile, Nazi SS murdered his father and brothers who had remained in Lithuania. He knew anxious times marked by the heresies of National Socialism and Fascism. He found God by excluding him. This business of otherness. We desire assurance, brothers and sisters. If we cannot have presence, we'll settle for absence.

3.

A young monk of some means systematically, night-by-night, visited each prostitute in the city. After he had paid for his time, he would tell the young women to the rest themselves for the evening, asking only that they pray for his salvation. He lived with scandal, derision, contempt. Dyed in grace.

"Putas quid est Deus? Putas qualis est Deus? Quidquid finxeris, non est; quidquid cogatione comprehenderis, non est. Sed ut aliquid gustu accipias, Deus caritas est; Caritas qua diligimus."

Words written during the suffering and subsequent death of John Paul II, the Pope of Rome

March 31–April 3, 2005

Thursday morning: My four-year-old son Aidan disappeared from our farm. His brothers Brendan, Dylan, and Tommy and his older sister Mae helped me search the fields, the woods and creek beds. Looked in the dust of Clark Road for fresh tire prints. We cried his name until we were hoarse. My wife found him locked in the van, crying. How many times had I walked past him, his name in my mouth, though I could neither see nor hear him behind the glass? He had gone to a retrieve a holy card, the Archangel Michael wrestling darkness to the ground.

Thursday evening: A young woman, her face like a portrait on a Greco-Egyptian sarcophagus, played Vaughn Williams' sublime "The Lark Ascending," while I sat on the stairs of an auditorium made electric with suspended breath. Her violin spoke in tongues of longing, the arpeggios evocative of a spiritual and eternal desire.

Friday morning: A marsh hawk stood on the embankment of the creek, pulling the meat from a hognose snake into thin red strips with his beak. He refused to move when I neared. Gave me a glance and ripped more flesh.

Friday afternoon: Sat with five mothers of ballerinas in the claustrophobic vestibule of my daughter's ballet school among discarded tennis shoes, pink sweaters, and dance bags, surrounded by dust-covered plastic ferns and photos of blowsy *Madame* in Russia when she was lithe and in her prime. One woman, a powerbroker named Kellie, told of a little boy's death. Only seven, no one knew of his congenital heart problem: on Sunday he told the babysitter his heart hurt and then died in her arms.

Friday night: Fell asleep reading science fiction: Yahweh and the Shekinah meeting as schoolchildren, trying to discover whose world is the real one. It's too bad about the Gnostics' misunderstanding of the flesh: they could really tell a good story.

Saturday morning: Drove to the dump. Cardboard boxes, tin, wine bottles. On the CD player: Kate Bush's "Running up That Hill" and the Derek and the Dominos version of the Hendrix masterpiece "Little Wing." The pain of others inspires us to better living. To better eating, laughter, weeping.

Saturday, late afternoon: Czeslaw Milosz's *New and Collected Poems, 1931–2001* vanished from its perch atop the piano. It could be found nowhere. I accused my wife of throwing it out. Such indignation! She told me to shut up and pray to St Anthony. Prayed, but pretended it was my idea. Crouched near a bookshelf for one last look. Lost my balance and put out my hand to steady myself. It landed on the book in question, what my mother calls a "signal grace." Beneath the volume: a holy card of St Augustine, ex-professor of rhetoric, reformed profligate, and lapsed Manichaean.

Sunday morning: My seventh child, Isabel Sophia, was baptized and chrismated according to the Rite of the Byzantine Catholic Church. She cried when Father Cyril plunged her into the font, laughed as he touched her heart with oil sweetened by roses.

Sunday night: Slept. Woke at two and checked the kids in their beds. Slept again.

Dat rosa mel apibus

The swarm lighted upon the box elder branch that hung just over the creek, rejoicing in the queen. I shook the bees into a paper grocery bag and delivered them to a new hive, where they poured themselves, graciously, as we all do, into the recesses. Children in a troubled world. I am by your side. I remember.

The crocus has a pistil, stigma, three petals, three sepals. Tulip, six. Strawberry, five. Hibiscus, four. This rose has seven. Multiflora. Floribunda. Remontant. Perpetual.

I could never light enough candles, never say enough prayers. This is the *mysterion*. Above and beyond all blessings.

Opticks

I.

J. W. von Goethe discovers the world

Newton's prism catches light,
A thing we cannot grasp,
And breaks it open to blood
In the dialectic of science.
But the poet disregards
The prism's taut methodology
And peers through the triangle
At a *world* refracted.
In light, he sees nothing.
Nothing in darkness.
Only at the edges, the boundary
Between these dual abstractions, is
The spectrum forced into a tenuous
Existence, a quiet violence wresting red
And amber from repose with violet and blue.
Colour, sayeth Sir Isaac,
Is but a nothing:
Vibration, accident, absence.
And so we believe
In nothing we see.

II.

July 1989. London. The Tate Gallery.

Rossetti's elaborate canvases burst
With voluptuous virgins, pure as apples.
Waterhouse's lady stares from the canvas:
She is already pale, already abandoned
To the river's disconcerting shadows.

Turner's visions: gales of red and black
And of fire indistinguishable from the sea.
Then I saw leaves from the Prophetic Books
Of William Blake, printer. Lambeth.

His astounding blue:
Like the cerulean ring
Around a mourning dove's eye.
At eighteen I saw a flash
From a solar eclipse reflected
In the black hood of a pickup truck.
The ghost of the sun remained
In my field of vision three days.
But the poet's blue resides in me still.
Strange that I cannot recall the images,
Whether they included the demiurge
Urizen scratching the Face of the Deep
With a compass pin; angelic Satan,
His wings still filled with infant light;
Or the joyful promise of a Glad Day.
I see only blue.

                    Alongside one print
The curators had posted a strip of paper,
A scale to limn the degrees by which
The pigments had degenerated since 1804
When Blake baptized his prints with color.
Though the engravings still held angels,
The light had faded them.
What was color before the angel fell?
What is darkness?

III.

Corpus poetarum

Language is a body, hardened corpuscles of light that do nothing we
ask of them. Phosphorus and calcium lie in bones: light and stone.
Thus language. We dream in tongues unknown to us: *koine* at the
threshold of sleep; Latin hexameters as if chanted to gods. (You have
heard them, but only listened when they called your name.) Voices are
clumsy, verses fall to corruption. You tumble the same words together
in your mouth, over and over again, as if coins of value. Wind the
sheet over your face. Close your eyes. It is time to surrender your
words. If you are lucky, St Thérèse of Lisieux will come to you:
Réveillé-toi, she will whisper. *Viens pour entendre mes os.* For this is
poetry: when saints intrude upon the sleep of the dead, and even bones
can sing.

Answer, possibly to Virgil

I spent most of the morning translating a poem called
Copa, a piece from the juvenilia of Virgil,
Written, say the critics, before he had become himself.
The poem consists of a wise barmaid's practical advice
To a young man much overburdened with "important things."
Look, she tells him, at the sensual beauty of the world:
The abundance of chestnuts and almonds, plums and apples,
Delicate cheeses and the delights of even cheap wine;
How joyful to hear the strains of a shepherd's pipe resound
Over fields while a nymph sings under a leafy arbor.
Embrace these things as you would the body of a lover,
For beneath the skin is always the presence of a skull.
Death plucks your ear. "Live," he says, "I am coming."

I know it's obvious, but I need to remark here
That the laurelled Augustan did not write this poem
In the early years of the twenty-first century,
In Michigan during a frigid spring when snow piles,
Stuffed with empty liquor bottles, bounced checks, and want ads,
Clung to the ground and to the margins of parking lots;
That he'd never driven north on I-75
To see the Rouge Plant release its spirit to the winds
And dump its filth into the river that shares its name;
That he did not know Detroit, a city without trees,
A city of suffering, where the dead homes of dead
Autoworkers speckle the landscape like bullet holes;
That he was not Catholic in the waxy days of Lent,
Bent on fasting and the contemplation of his sins.
Virgil, if it was you, and you, my silent reader,
How should I have this poem end? What's the fitting coda?
Life plucks your ear. "Die," he says, "I am coming."